I Love The Woman I Am Becoming! I am Fighting Hard to Stay Her!

A Book Journal of Healing and Wholeness

I Love The Woman I Am Becoming!
I am Fighting Hard to Stay Her!

**A Book Journal of Healing
and Wholeness**

© 2025 Alisa L. Grace

All rights reserved.

No part of this book may be reproduced in any form or by any electronic or mechanical means, including information storage and retrieval systems, without permission in writing from the publisher.

Self-Published by

Alisa L. Grace

Sanford, FL 32771

ISBN: 978-1-966129-15-8

First Edition

Printed in the United States of America

Library of Congress Cataloging-in-Publication Data

Grace, Alisa L.

Title of the Book: I Love the Woman I Am Becoming: I Am Fighting Hard to Stay Her Book

Library of Congress Control Number: 2024923780

Disclaimer: The views expressed in this book are those of the author and do not necessarily reflect any organizations or individuals mentioned.

Acknowledgments: The author wishes to thank God, Her Husband (Linion), Victory Temple of God, Florida SPECS, Unity Youth Association, All About Serving You, Angels-ANJ Events, NordeVest, and Love & Create Life for their support and contributions.

This journal is a tribute to the warriors, the survivors, and the women who refuse to be defined by their struggles. It's a space to reclaim your power, rewrite your story, and rise into the fullness of your God-given potential.

Table of Contents

Introduction 9

I Love The Woman I Am Becoming Book Journal: Is It Right for You? 11

Welcome, Beautiful Soul 13

Dreams and Aspirations 15

How to Use This Book Journal 17

Transformation Begins Now: 19

   Start with the woman in the mirror 20

Sacred Sanctuary 21

   Healing Waters 1: Reflecting Pool 23

   Healing Waters 2: Inner Springs 24

   Healing Waters 3: Cleansing Rains: 25

   The Cleaning of the Body 26

Sacred Sanctuary: The Cleaning of the Body 27

   Healing Waters 1: Nurturing the Temple 29

   Healing Waters 2: Movement as Medicine 30

   Healing Waters 3: The Gift of Rest 31

   Recreate the Heart 32

Sacred Sanctuary: Recreate the Heart 33

   Healing Waters 1: Tenderly Tending Wounds 35

   Healing Waters 2: The Path of Forgiveness 36

   Healing Waters 3: Cultivating Self-Compassion 37

   Transformation 38

Sacred Sanctuary: Transformation 39

   Healing Waters 1: Envisioning Your Highest Self 41

   Healing Waters 2: Setting Goals with Intention 42

   Healing Waters 3: Nurturing Motivation and Perseverance 43

   Love Who You Are 44

Sacred Sanctuary: Love Who You Are **45**

    Healing Waters 1: Celebrating Your Journey 47

    Healing Waters 2: Gratitude and Self-Appreciation 48

    Healing Waters 3: Embracing Imperfections 49

    Fight to Remain Beautiful 50

Sacred Sanctuary: Fight to Remain Beautiful **51**

    Healing Waters 1: Cultivating Resilience 53

    Healing Waters 2: Overcoming Obstacles 54

    Healing Waters 3: Affirmations of Strength 55

    Extra Note Sections: A Tapestry of Your Journey 56

Final Healing Waters: **57**

A Final Word of Encouragement and Reflection **59**

Meet the Author: Alisa Grace **61**

Introduction

Dearest Woman, Warrior, Survivor,

Welcome to a sacred space, a haven carved out just for you. Within these pages lies a path toward healing, restoration, and the glorious revival of your spirit.

This journal is more than ink and paper; it's a gentle hand reaching out, a whispered promise of hope. It recognizes the battles you've fought, the scars you carry, and the strength that has carried you through. It is a testament to your resilience and an invitation to embrace the transformative journey that awaits.

Together, we will delve into the depths of your being, unearthing the hidden treasures within. We will nurture your inner beauty, reignite your strength, and unleash the boundless potential that lies dormant. This is a space to shed the weight of the past, reclaim your power, and rise like the phoenix from the ashes of your struggles.

As we journey together, let these words from Scripture be our guiding light:

"He heals the brokenhearted and binds up their wounds."
- Psalm 147:3

"The Lord is close to the brokenhearted and saves those who are crushed in spirit."
- Psalm 34:18

"Forget the former things; do not dwell on the past. See, I am doing a new thing! Now it springs up; do you not perceive it?"
- Isaiah 43:18-19

Know that you are not alone. You are cherished, worthy, and capable of extraordinary things. This journal is a sanctuary where you can lay down your burdens, find solace in self-discovery, and rise to embrace the woman you are becoming.

With love and unwavering support,

Your Guide on this Sacred Journey

I Love The Woman I Am Becoming Book Journal: Is It Right for You?

This short survey is designed to help you determine if this journal is the perfect companion for your journey of self-discovery and transformation. Answer honestly, and let your intuition guide you.

1. Personal Reflection:

Are you a woman who has experienced struggles or challenges in your life?

Do you desire healing, restoration, and a renewed sense of purpose?

Are you open to exploring your inner world and embracing your true self?

Are you seeking a safe space to express your emotions and thoughts without judgment?

2. Spiritual Connection:

Do you believe in a higher power or universal energy that guides and supports you?

Are you interested in deepening your spiritual connection and exploring your faith?

Do you find comfort and inspiration in the wisdom of nature?

3. Journaling Practice:

Do you enjoy writing and reflecting on your experiences?

Are you seeking a guided journal with prompts and activities to support your self-discovery?

Do you want a journal that combines both natural and spiritual perspectives?

4. Desired Outcomes:

Are you ready to embark on a journey of self-love and transformation?

Do you want to cultivate greater self-awareness, resilience, and inner strength?

Are you seeking a tangible tool to support your personal growth and healing?

If you answered "yes" to most of these questions, I Love The Woman I Am Becoming may be your perfect journal!

This journal empowers and inspires women on their paths to wholeness. It offers a safe space for self-reflection, spiritual connection, and self-love cultivation. If you're ready to embrace your journey of becoming, this journal is here to guide and support you every step of the way.

Welcome, Beautiful Soul

"The wound is the place where the Light enters you." - Rumi

As you embark on this transformative journey, may you find solace, strength, and the radiant light within.

Your Name: _____

Date of Beginning: _____

Dreams and Aspirations

Take a moment to breathe deeply and connect with your heart's desires. What hopes and dreams do you hold for yourself? What seeds of possibility are yearning to bloom?

Write freely, allowing your aspirations to flow onto the page. Embrace the vulnerability of this moment and dare to dream big. Your dreams are the whispers of your soul, guiding you toward your highest potential.

How to Use This Book Journal

Embrace the Journey:

Sacred Space: Find a quiet and comfortable space to dedicate uninterrupted time to journaling. Light a candle, play soft music, or surround yourself with natural elements to create a peaceful atmosphere.

Open Heart: Approach each section with an open heart and a willingness to explore your inner world. Let go of judgment and embrace vulnerability.

Divine Connection: Remember that this journal is not just a tool for self-reflection but also an invitation to deepen your connection with God. Invite His presence into your journaling time through prayer or quiet contemplation.

No Rules: No right or wrong way to use this journal exists. Write freely, doodle, draw, or express yourself authentically.

Navigating the Sections:

Read the Introduction and Welcome Pages: Begin by immersing yourself in the journal's purpose and message. Take time to fill out the welcome pages, setting your intentions for this transformative journey.

Explore Each Section: Move through the sections at your own pace, allowing yourself ample time to reflect on the prompts and engage in the suggested activities.

Sacred Sanctuary and Healing Waters: These sections facilitate deeper introspection and spiritual connection. Approach them with an open heart and a willingness to explore your relationship with God and your inner wisdom.

Extra Note Sections: Utilize the blank pages at the end for additional reflections, creative expression, or goal setting.

Additional Tips:

Consistency: Aim for regular journaling sessions, even if it's just for a few minutes each day. Consistency will help you build momentum and deepen your self-discovery.

Honesty and Vulnerability: Be honest with yourself as you write. Allow your true feelings and thoughts to flow onto the page without censorship.

Self-Compassion: Approach yourself with kindness and understanding. Remember that healing and transformation take time, and it's okay to have setbacks or moments of doubt.

Celebrate Your Progress: Acknowledge and celebrate your growth and achievements along the way.

May this journal be a source of comfort, inspiration, and empowerment as you embark on the beautiful journey of loving the woman you are becoming.

With continued love and unwavering support,

Your Guide on this Sacred Journey

Transformation Begins Now:

Start with the woman in the mirror

Gaze deeply into your own eyes, beloved. In this mirror lies a reflection of resilience, strength, and untold beauty. This section invites you to embark on a journey of self-discovery, peel back the layers, and embrace the woman who gazes back at you.

Through guided prompts, we'll navigate the landscape of your inner world. We'll uncover the hidden gems of your strengths and celebrate the unique tapestry of your being. Together, we'll challenge the voices of self-doubt, replacing them with affirmations that nourish your spirit and ignite your self-worth.

As you explore, remember that nature is a mirror reflecting your own magnificence. Just as a flower blooms in its own time, you will also unfold in perfect rhythm. Connect with the wisdom of the natural world, finding solace and inspiration in its ever-present beauty.

And if you seek more profound guidance, turn inward. Listen to the whispers of your intuition, the divine spark that resides within. Connect with your higher power, inner wisdom, or the universal energy sustaining us all.

This is your sacred space to honor the woman in the mirror, to love her unconditionally, and to embark on the transformative journey of becoming.

Sacred Sanctuary

Healing Waters 1: Reflecting Pool

Reflection: Close your eyes and envision the woman you were five years ago. What challenges did she face? What strengths did she possess? How has she grown and evolved into the woman you are today?

Scripture: "For we are God's handiwork, created in Christ Jesus to do good works, which God prepared in advance for us to do." - Ephesians 2:10

Mantra: I am a masterpiece in progress, continually shaped by divine hands.

Affirmation: I am proud of my journey and the woman I am becoming.

_____

_____

_____

_____

_____

_____

_____

_____

_____

_____

_____

_____

_____

_____

Healing Waters 2: Inner Springs

Reflection: What limiting beliefs or negative self-talk do you often hear in your mind? Write them down without judgment. Now, challenge each one with a truth about your inherent worth and potential.

Scripture: "I praise you because I am fearfully and wonderfully made; your works are wonderful, I know that full well." - Psalm 139:14

Mantra: I am fearfully and wonderfully made, a testament to divine creativity.

Affirmation: I release limiting beliefs and embrace the truth of my inherent worth.

_____

_____

_____

_____

_____

_____

_____

_____

_____

_____

_____

_____

_____

Healing Waters 3: Cleansing Rains:

Reflection: What are the three qualities you admire most about yourself? How do these qualities contribute to your unique beauty and strength?

Scripture: "Charm is deceptive, and beauty is fleeting, but a woman who fears the Lord is to be praised." - Proverbs 31:30

Mantra: My true beauty lies in my character, my connection to the divine.

Affirmation: I am beautiful inside and out, radiating the light of my spirit.

_____
_____
_____
_____
_____
_____
_____
_____
_____
_____
_____
_____
_____

The Cleaning of the Body

This section is a gentle invitation to honor your physical vessel, recognizing it as a temple deserving of love and care. It's a space to explore self-care practices that nourish your body, mind, and spirit. These pages reveal the transformative power of healthy habits, mindful movement, and intentional rest.

As you embark on this journey of cleansing and renewal, remember that nature offers a bounty of healing resources. From soothing herbs and fragrant essential oils to the restorative power of the earth itself, let the natural world guide you toward balance and well-being.

And as you cultivate a deeper connection with your body, tune in to its innate wisdom. Mindful eating, yoga, and meditation can help you tap into its subtle messages, fostering a harmonious relationship between your physical and spiritual selves. This is a sacred journey of rediscovering your body's inherent strength and beauty, honoring it as a vessel for your radiant spirit.

Sacred Sanctuary: The Cleaning of the Body

Healing Waters 1: Nurturing the Temple

Reflection: How do you currently care for your physical body? Are there areas where you feel you could show more love and attention? What self-care practices bring you joy and nourishment?

Scripture: "Do you not know that your bodies are temples of the Holy Spirit, who is in you, whom you have received from God? You are not your own; you were bought at a price. Therefore, honor God with your bodies." - 1 Corinthians 6:19-20

Mantra: My body is a sacred temple deserving of love, respect, and care.

Affirmation: I commit to nourishing my body with wholesome choices and mindful practices.

_____
_____
_____
_____
_____
_____
_____
_____
_____
_____
_____
_____
_____
_____

Healing Waters 2: Movement as Medicine

Reflection: How does movement currently play a role in your life? What forms of exercise or physical activity bring you joy and energy? What gentle ways can you incorporate more movement into your daily routine?

Scripture: "She is clothed with strength and dignity; she can laugh at the days to come." - Proverbs 31:25

Mantra: My body is strong and capable, and movement is a celebration of its power.

Affirmation: I embrace movement as a source of joy, vitality, and strength.

_____
_____
_____
_____
_____
_____
_____
_____
_____
_____
_____
_____
_____

Healing Waters 3: The Gift of Rest

Reflection: How do you currently prioritize rest in your life? What activities or practices help you unwind and recharge? What are some ways you can create a more restful environment for yourself?

Scripture: "Come to me, all you who are weary and burdened, and I will give you rest." - Matthew 11:28

Mantra: Rest is not a luxury but a necessity for my well-being.

Affirmation: I give myself permission to rest, recharge, and renew my spirit.

_____
_____
_____
_____
_____
_____
_____
_____
_____
_____
_____
_____

Recreate the Heart

This section invites you to embark on a profound journey of healing and transformation, where the wounds of the past can be gently tended and released. It's a space to acknowledge your emotional baggage, explore forgiveness for yourself and others, and cultivate a deep sense of self-compassion and kindness.

As you delve into this sacred work, draw inspiration from nature's resilience. Just as a forest regenerates after a fire or a river carves a new path after a flood, your heart can also heal and flourish. Embrace nature's metaphors as a reminder of your innate capacity for renewal and growth.

Explore spiritual practices that connect you with the heart's energy center alongside these natural reflections. Loving-kindness meditation, prayer, and other heart-opening techniques can help you cultivate a deep love and compassion for yourself and the world around you. This is a journey of reclaiming your heart's power, allowing it to beat with renewed strength, joy, and unwavering love.

Sacred Sanctuary: Recreate the Heart

Healing Waters 1: Tenderly Tending Wounds

Reflection: Identify a past wound or emotional hurt that you still carry. Describe the experience, its emotions, and how it may still affect you today.

Scripture: "He heals the brokenhearted and binds up their wounds." - Psalm 147:3

Mantra: I release the past and embrace the healing power of God's love.

Affirmation: I am safe to feel my emotions and allow my heart to heal.

_____
_____
_____
_____
_____
_____
_____
_____
_____
_____
_____
_____
_____
_____
_____

Healing Waters 2: The Path of Forgiveness

Reflection: Is there someone you need to forgive, including yourself? Write a letter of forgiveness, expressing your feelings and releasing any resentment or anger you may hold.

Scripture: "For if you forgive other people when they sin against you, your heavenly Father will also forgive you." - Matthew 6:14

Mantra: Forgiveness sets me free and opens my heart to love.

Affirmation: I choose forgiveness, releasing the past, and embracing peace.

_____

_____

_____

_____

_____

_____

_____

_____

_____

_____

_____

_____

_____

_____

Healing Waters 3: Cultivating Self-Compassion

Reflection: How do you typically speak to yourself during struggle or self-doubt? Write down some of your common negative self-talk patterns. Now, rewrite these statements with words of kindness, understanding, and compassion.

Scripture: "As a father has compassion on his children, so the Lord has compassion on those who fear him." - Psalm 103:13

Mantra: I am worthy of love and compassion, just as I am.

Affirmation: I speak to myself with kindness and embrace my imperfections with love.

_____
_____
_____
_____
_____
_____
_____
_____
_____
_____
_____
_____
_____

Transformation

This section is an invitation to embrace the beautiful metamorphosis process, shed old limitations, and emerge as the radiant butterfly you were always meant to be. It's a space to envision your highest self, set inspiring goals for personal growth, and create actionable plans to bring those dreams to fruition.

As you navigate this transformative journey, remember the awe-inspiring metamorphosis of a caterpillar into a butterfly. It's a powerful reminder that change, even when challenging, can lead to extraordinary beauty and freedom. Let nature's example inspire you to embrace the unfolding of your own transformation, trusting in the divine timing of your growth.

Alongside these natural reflections, explore spiritual practices that can support your transformation journey. Prayer, vision boards, and other intentional rituals can help you connect with your deepest desires, align with your purpose, and manifest your dreams into reality. This is a time to tap into your spiritual strength, allowing it to fuel your motivation, perseverance, and unwavering belief in your limitless potential.

Sacred Sanctuary: Transformation

Healing Waters 1: Envisioning Your Highest Self

Reflection: Close your eyes and envision the woman you aspire to be. What qualities does she embody? How does she live her life? What impact does she have on the world around her?

Scripture: "For I know the plans I have for you," declares the Lord, "plans to prosper you and not to harm you, plans to give you hope and a future." - Jeremiah 29:11

Mantra: I am aligned with God's divine plan for my life, and my highest self is unfolding.

Affirmation: I embrace my potential and step into the woman I am becoming.

_____

_____

_____

_____

_____

_____

_____

_____

_____

_____

_____

_____

_____

Healing Waters 2: Setting Goals with Intention

Reflection: What specific goals do you want to achieve in the next six months, one year, and five years? Break down each goal into smaller, actionable steps.

Scripture: "Commit to the Lord whatever you do, and he will establish your plans." - Proverbs 16:3

Mantra: My goals are rooted in God's will, and I trust in His guidance.

Affirmation: I am committed to taking inspired action toward my dreams.

_____

_____

_____

_____

_____

_____

_____

_____

_____

_____

_____

_____

_____

_____

Healing Waters 3: Nurturing Motivation and Perseverance

Reflection: What challenges or obstacles might you encounter on your transformation journey? How will you overcome them? What practices or affirmations will help you stay motivated and persevere?

Scripture: "I can do all this through him who gives me strength." - Philippians 4:13

Mantra: I am empowered by God's strength to overcome any challenge.

Affirmation: I am resilient, persistent, and capable of achieving my goals.

_____
_____
_____
_____
_____
_____
_____
_____
_____
_____
_____
_____
_____

Love Who You Are

This section is a joyous celebration of the incredible woman you have become through your journey of healing and transformation. It's a space to bask in the radiance of your own being, to acknowledge your strengths, resilience, and the unique beauty that shines from within.

As you reflect on your journey, remember that every flower in a garden is beautiful in its own way. Just as nature embraces diversity and celebrates each blossom's unique qualities, so should you embrace your own individuality and imperfections.

This section also invites you to connect with the boundless love and acceptance that flows from your higher power. God's love is unconditional, embracing you thoroughly and completely, just as you are. Allow yourself to receive this love, to feel its warmth and comfort, and to know that you are cherished beyond measure.

Sacred Sanctuary: Love Who You Are

Healing Waters 1: Celebrating Your Journey

Reflection: Take a moment to acknowledge all you have overcome and achieved on your journey thus far. What are you most proud of? What lessons have you learned? How have you grown and transformed?

Scripture: "For we are God's handiwork, created in Christ Jesus to do good works, which God prepared in advance for us to do." - Ephesians 2:10

Mantra: I am a masterpiece created with divine purpose and intention.

Affirmation: I celebrate my journey and all that I have become.

_____
_____
_____
_____
_____
_____
_____
_____
_____
_____
_____
_____
_____

Healing Waters 2: Gratitude and Self-Appreciation

Reflection: Make a list of 10 things you are grateful for in your life right now. Then, write down 5 qualities you appreciate about yourself.

Scripture: "Give thanks in all circumstances; for this is God's will for you in Christ Jesus." - 1 Thessalonians 5:18

Mantra: Gratitude fills my heart and opens me to God's blessings.

Affirmation: I am grateful for my life and all the gifts it holds.

_____

_____

_____

_____

_____

_____

_____

_____

_____

_____

_____

_____

_____

_____

Healing Waters 3: Embracing Imperfections

Reflection: What imperfections or perceived flaws do you struggle to accept about yourself? How can you reframe these imperfections as part of your unique beauty and story?

Scripture: "But he said to me, 'My grace is sufficient for you, for my power is made perfect in weakness.' Therefore I will boast all the more gladly about my weaknesses so that Christ's power may rest on me." - 2 Corinthians 12:9

Mantra: My imperfections are part of my story, and God's grace is sufficient.

Affirmation: I embrace my imperfections with love and acceptance.

_____
_____
_____
_____
_____
_____
_____
_____
_____
_____
_____
_____

Fight to Remain Beautiful

This section is a call to arms, a reminder that the journey of self-love and transformation is ongoing. It's a space to cultivate the inner strength and resilience to face life's challenges gracefully and determined. Here, you'll explore strategies for maintaining self-love even in the face of adversity, identify potential obstacles to your growth, and develop affirmations that empower you to rise above any challenge.

As you navigate life's inevitable storms, look to nature for inspiration. The mighty oak stands tall against the wind, the desert flower blooms in the harshest conditions, and the salmon swims upstream against all odds. These examples of nature's perseverance remind us that we, too, possess an unyielding spirit and can overcome any obstacle.

In moments of doubt or despair, turn to your spiritual connection for strength and support. Prayer, meditation, and other practices can help you tap into the divine wellspring of resilience that resides within. This is a time to fortify your faith, draw strength from your spiritual beliefs, and remember that you are never alone on this journey.

Sacred Sanctuary: Fight to Remain Beautiful

Healing Waters 1: Cultivating Resilience

Reflection: What challenges or setbacks do you anticipate facing in the future? How can you mentally, emotionally, and spiritually prepare yourself to navigate these challenges with grace and strength?

Scripture: "I have told you these things, so that in me you may have peace. In this world, you will have trouble. But take heart! I have overcome the world." - John 16:33

Mantra: I am resilient and capable of overcoming any challenge with God's help.

Affirmation: I face life's challenges with courage, strength, and unwavering faith.

_____

_____

_____

_____

_____

_____

_____

_____

_____

_____

_____

_____

_____

_____

Healing Waters 2: Overcoming Obstacles

Reflection: Identify any internal or external obstacles that might hinder your growth and transformation. What steps can you take to overcome these obstacles? Who or what can you turn to for support?

Scripture: "No temptation has overtaken you except what is common to mankind. And God is faithful; he will not let you be tempted beyond what you can bear. But when you are tempted, he will also provide a way out so that you can endure it." - 1 Corinthians 10:13

Mantra: With God's help, I can overcome any obstacle that stands in my way.

Affirmation: I am resourceful, determined, and capable of finding solutions.

_____

_____

_____

_____

_____

_____

_____

_____

_____

_____

_____

_____

_____

Healing Waters 3: Affirmations of Strength

Reflection: Write down five affirmations that resonate with you and speak to your inner strength, resilience, and determination. Repeat these affirmations daily, especially when facing challenges or self-doubt.

Scripture: "Be strong and courageous. Do not be afraid or terrified because of them, for the Lord your God goes with you; he will never leave you nor forsake you." - Deuteronomy 31:6

Mantra: I am strong, courageous, and never alone. God is always with me.

Affirmation: I am filled with divine strength and unwavering determination.

_____
_____
_____
_____
_____
_____
_____
_____
_____
_____
_____
_____
_____

Extra Note Sections: A Tapestry of Your Journey

As you reach the final pages of this journal, may they serve as a canvas for the ongoing tapestry of your journey. Here, you'll find blank pages awaiting your personal touch, a space for continued reflection, creative expression, or the setting of new intentions. Capture fleeting thoughts, doodle your heart's desires, or pen letters of love to your future self.

Within these pages, create a treasury of inspiration. Gather your favorite quotes, affirmations, or messages that have touched your soul along the way. Let these words serve as guiding lights, illuminating your path as you grow and evolve.

As you close this chapter, remember that self-discovery and transformation are lifelong. May this journal be a cherished companion, a testament to your resilience, and a reminder of the boundless love and strength within you.

_____

_____

_____

_____

_____

_____

_____

_____

_____

_____

_____

Final Healing Waters:

What seeds of intention will you plant today, knowing they will blossom into the beautiful reality of your tomorrow? Embrace the ever-unfolding journey of becoming and continue to nurture the incredible woman you are. The world awaits your radiance.

_____
_____
_____
_____
_____
_____
_____
_____
_____
_____
_____
_____
_____
_____
_____
_____
_____

A Final Word of Encouragement and Reflection

As you journey through the pages of "I Love The Woman I Am Becoming," may you find solace, strength, and inspiration in the words and reflections within. Remember, this journal is more than just a collection of prompts; it's a sacred space where your heart and spirit can unfold.

Throughout these sections, we've woven together the wisdom of nature and the power of faith, inviting you to connect with the earth beneath your feet and the divine presence within. May the gentle guidance and empowering affirmations nurture your soul and illuminate your path toward healing, restoration, and revival.

As you complete each section, take a moment to reflect on your growth and transformation. Celebrate your victories, acknowledge your challenges, and embrace the beautiful tapestry of your journey. Remember, you are a masterpiece in the making, continually shaped by the loving hands of your Creator.

May this journal constantly remind you of your inherent worth, your boundless potential, and the unwavering love that surrounds you. As you turn the final page, carry the lessons and insights you've gained into the world, shining your light brightly and inspiring others to embrace their own journey of becoming.

With love and blessings,

Your Guide on this Sacred Journey

Meet the Author: Alisa Grace

Alisa Grace is a passionate advocate for women's empowerment and healing, dedicated to inspiring others through her own journey of overcoming adversity. With over 30 years of marriage, she credits her husband as her greatest supporter, enriching her life with love and partnership. As a devoted mother and grandmother, Alisa embodies the values of family and connection, grounding her work in the deep love she shares with her loved ones.

Drawing from her experiences as a local missionary and transformational life coach, Alisa has crafted "I Love The Woman I Am Becoming," a journal that reflects her belief in the resilience of the human spirit and the boundless potential within each individual. Her writing is infused with compassion and gentle strength, inviting readers to embark on their own journeys of self-discovery and healing.

A retired school administrator, Alisa combines her love for learning and personal growth with a holistic approach to transformation, weaving together natural and spiritual perspectives. She finds solace and inspiration in nature, often spending her days hiking, meditating, or basking in the warmth of the sun. Her faith serves as a cornerstone of her life, providing her with unwavering strength and guidance.

Alisa's greatest hope is that her journal will be a beacon of hope for women who have faced struggles, reminding them that they are not alone and possess the inner strength to heal, transform, and fully embrace their authentic selves.

"Embark on a transformative journey of self-discovery and healing with this journal designed specifically for women who are struggling yet fighting to become the women God has designed them to be. Within these pages, you'll find:

Sacred Sanctuary: A space to connect with your inner self and discover your true potential.
Healing Waters: Guided prompts to heal past wounds, release emotional baggage, and cultivate self-compassion. Transformative Reflections: Space for envisioning goals, setting intentions, and embracing personal growth. Love Who You Are: Affirmations and practices to celebrate your unique beauty and embrace your imperfections. Fight to Remain Beautiful: Strategies for overcoming challenges, maintaining self-love, and staying true to your path.

This journal is your battleground, a place to unleash your warrior spirit and claim your rightful place in the world. It's a space for self-reflection, empowerment, and transformation.

Step into the pages of "I Love The Woman I Am Becoming: I'm Fighting Hard to Stay Her!" and embark on a journey that will change your life forever."

Call to Action:

"Embrace the woman you are becoming. Start your journey of transformation today!

www.ingramcontent.com/pod-product-compliance
Lightning Source LLC
LaVergne TN
LVHW061326060426
835510LV00017B/1939